Recollections

of

Rear Admiral Etheridge Grant

U. S. Navy (Retired)

U. S. Naval Institute

Annapolis, Maryland

1971

This manuscript is the result of a tape recorded interview with Rear Admiral Etheridge Grant, USN (Ret.) at his home in Ojai, California on October 17, 1970. The interview was conducted by Commander Etta Belle Kitchen, USN (Ret.) for the Oral History Office in the U. S. Naval Institute.

Only minor emendations and corrections have been made to the manuscript. The reader is asked to bear in mind therefore that he is reading a transcript of the spoken word rather than the written word.

DECLARATION OF TRUST

The undersigned does hereby appoint and designate as his (her) Trustee herein, the Secretary-Treasurer and Publisher of the United States Naval Institute to perform and discharge the following duties, powers, and privileges in connection with the possession and use of a certain taped interview between the undersigned and the Oral History Department of the United States Naval Institute.

(1) As an <u>Open</u> transcript. It may be read (or the tape audited) by qualified researchers upon presentation of proper credentials as determined by the Trustee.

(2) It is expressly understood that in giving this authorization, I am in no way precluded from placing such restrictions as I may desire upon use of the interview at any time during my lifetime, nor does this authorization in any way affect my rights to the copyright of any literary expressions that may be contained in the interview.

Witness my hand and seal this **6th** day of **February** 19**71**

Etheridge Grant

I hereby accept and consent to the foregoing Declaration of Trust and the powers therein conferred upon me as Trustee:

R E Bowler
Secretary-Treasurer and Publisher

Pers-E24-FSR:tlb
23 Aug 1956

REAR ADMIRAL ETHERIDGE GRANT, U. S. NAVY, RETIRED, 60388
PARTIAL TRANSCRIPT OF NAVAL SERVICE

17 Jun 1902	Born in Chicago, Illinois
14 Jun 1922	Midshipman, U. S. Navy
3 Jun 1926	Ensign, U. S. Navy
1 Jul 1948	Captain, U. S. Navy, to rank from 1 Aug 1943
30 Jun 1956	Rear Admiral, U. S. Navy having been specially Commended for performance of duty in actual combat
30 Jun 1956	Placed on the Retired List of the U. S. Navy

SHIPS AND STATIONS	FROM	TO
Naval Operations, Navy Dept. (Dufly)	May 1946	Jul 1947
Naval Operations, Navy Dept. (Chief, Civil Aviation Section)	Jul 1947	Sep 1949
U. S. Naval Air Station, Agana, Guam, M. I. (Commanding Officer)	Sep 1949	Jun 1950
Commander Fleet Air Guam (Commander FAW ONE)	Jun 1950	Mar 1951
Staff, Commander Fleet Air Alameda	Mar 1951	Aug 1951
National War College, Washington, D. C. (Student)	Aug 1951	Jun 1952
Office Foreign Military Affairs, Office, Sec of Defense, (Action Officer, Foreign Military Affairs)	Jun 1952	Oct 1953
Office, Asst. Sec of Defense, International Security Affairs, OFMA, (Chief, S. Asia and China Bn.)	Oct 1953	Sep 1954
Office of Foreign Military Affairs, Office of Sec. of Defense (Executive Officer to the Director, OFMA)	Sep 1954	Feb 1956
Office of the Asst. Sec. of Defense (International Security Affairs) (Asst. to the Military Advisor)	Feb 1956	Jun 1956

Home Town Address: 1517 Ynez Place, Coronado, California
Date and Place of Marriage: 3 May 1927, New York City, N. Y.
Wife's Maiden Name and Home Town: Margaret Babb of Homer, Illinois
Children/Dates of Birth: Margaret B. Grant: 25 Jan 1931

Father: John M. Grant
Mother's Maiden Name: Fanny S. Etheridge
Schools or Colleges attended: Lawrenceville School, Lawrenceville, N. J.

Interview #1 with Rear Admiral James Etheridge Grant, USN (Ret.)

Ojai, California October 17, 1970

Subject: Biography E. B. Kitchen, Cdr., USN (Ret.)

Q: I notice that one of your letters, Admiral, is signed Etheridge Grant, and yet I notice on another occasion it's James Grant. Which do you like to be called?

Admiral Grant: All my friends call me Jim. I happen to have been christened, believe it or not, James Henry Etheridge MacGregory Grant. That was entirely too long for the Navy so when I entered Annapolis my father entered me as Etheridge Grant but there happened to be a few old friends there who continued to call me Jim. Officially in the Navy I'm just Etheridge Grant.

Q: Would you give me some statistics to begin our interview?

Grant; I was born in Chicago in 1902 and I didn't like it there so at the tender age of about six months, I persuaded my family to move away. They moved to London, England and stayed there for about five years. We then came back to this country and I was brought up, until I went to Lawrenceville, in a place called Scarsdale, New York. I didn't graduate from Lawrenceville; I left there a year early to go to Annapolis so you can say I never graduated from high school. At Annapolis I graduated in 1926 and had two years regular line Navy and then I went to Pensacola

Grant # 1 - 2

and became a naval aviator and was in aviation until I retired in 1956.

Q: What year did you become a naval aviator?

Grant: I went to Pensacola in 1929 and became an aviator in 1930. In the 1930s I went back to Annapolis and had two or three years of post graduate work ending up in the University of Michigan, where I received a Master's Degree in science.

Q: After your graduation from Ann Arbor, you had some duties between then and the beginning of World War II. Was any one of them noteworthy?

Grant: It was just regular carrier duty. I was on the SARATOGA on a torpedo squadron for about three years. Then I got detached from there in '39. After leaving the SARATOGA, the torpedo squadron, I was sent to Pearl Harbor and I was in charge of the engine overhaul section of the A and R shop there at the naval air station. A and R is "Assembly and Repair." I believe they have another name for that now but it has to do with repairing planes and engines and overhauling planes that have either crashed or are ready for regular overhaul. It was interesting duty but no shore duty, to me, is very interesting. I much prefer sea duty.

I was transferred from Pearl Harbor in June of 1941 to commanding officer of the USS WILLIAM B. PRESTON in the Philippines. We were stationed at Cavite and I was there for about six months

Grant # 1 - 3 -

or so before the war started. We were patrolling the area around the Philippines looking for suspicious Japanese activity in all the little bays and inlets all over the Philippines.

Q: Where were you at the time of Pearl Harbor?

Grant: We happened to be stationed, at the moment, my ship and about six sea planes, in one of the southern Philippine Islands, Mindanao. We knew that war was imminent, and one morning about three a.m., we received a dispatch from the admiral in Manila saying very briefly and very succinctly, quote, "Japan has commenced hostilities. Govern yourself accordingly." We had no idea where Japan had commenced hostilities. We didn't know whether it was in San Francisco, or Panama, or Hawaii, or the Philippines, or where, so we didn't know just how to govern ourselves accordingly. I happened to have six planes anchored around me so the first thing I did was to up anchor and move about a mile away from the planes, so if we should be attacked the planes attacking us would not get both the ship and our planes at the same time.

Q: Had you previously had an operation order which you were to execute in the event of hostilities?

Grant: None whatsoever. It was all taken care of by that phrase "govern yourselves accordingly."

Q: Was the admiral Admiral Hart?

Grant: I really don't remember. He was in charge of the Western Pacific and it might very well of been Hart.

Q: What happened after you moved away from your planes?

Grant: It was getting to be daylight about that time. We dropped anchor about a mile away from the planes and we sent three planes on the usual patrol. We were patrolling various bays and inlets all around the southern Philippines looking for any suspicious activities. So we sent three planes out and dropped anchor. I rigged the anchor for slipping in an emergency so we could just knock off one link and the anchor would fall into the sea and we would be free. We wouldn't have to waste time bringing it up.

Just as we had finished rigging the anchor, the lookout reported some planes were coming towards us over the horizon. Immediately I ordered full speed ahead before I even knew what kinds they were. We started zigging and zagging and sure enough they turned out to be Japanese planes. There were two groups --one group appeared to be small dive bombers and fighters. The other group at a little higher altitude appeared to be horizontal bombers. The dive bombers came in first and attacked the three remaining planes on the water and sank them all in just a few minutes. The high altitude bombers (when I say high altitude --they were coming in rather low) attacked the ship. I had noticed that the horizontal bombers coming toward the ship were rather low and peculiarly enough they were coming in down wind, which is not usually the case with bombers. I had remembered that when I had been practicing my high altitude bombing from various directions that whenever I came in low and down wind, I had a tendency to over-shoot the target. Thinking that perhaps the Japanese were not any smarter than I was, (they were coming in on the beam) whenever I saw that they were at about what I considered the proper dropping angle, I turned into them, and it was very lucky that I did. I could have zagged instead of zigged. But I turned into them and sure enough all the bombs dropped over.

Q: Do you have any recollection of how many bombs were dropped?

Grant: I think each plane dropped one bomb and they were about six or seven planes in each group. After they sunk our planes, the fighter planes left and disappeared. I slowed down, after the horizontal bombers had made about three runs, they also left and we figured they'd gone back to their carrier to get refueled. I put a boat in the water with orders to pick up the crew of the planes which were swimming around and take them to shore and wait until we returned. As we were zigging and zagging, during these three runs, we had seen heading for the open sea. As soon as the horizontal bombers had left, we returned and picked up our plane crews. Luckily there was only one killed and one or two wounded.

Our planes, of course, fired back at the dive bombers but all they had was just fifty caliber guns and they didn't do much good. In fact that's all we had on the ship.

Q: What type of ship was the PRESTON?

Grant: The PRESTON was an old four stacker destroyer which had been converted to a sea plane tender. They had taken out two of the four boilers and turned the space into living quarters for the crew.

Q: What speed did she have?

Grant: At full speed we could still make about twenty-five knots. It was fairly fast.

Q: How long did the attack take?

Grant: It's a little hard to remember. Making three runs, probably ten minutes each run. It seemed quite a while --probably a little longer than that. When the attack was over, I heard some of the boys on the bridge discussing the attack, and one of them said to the quartermaster, "Gee, I sure was scared." The quartermaster said, "I was too. It's a good thing the old man wasn't scared." I couldn't help but overhear that and I said, "Listen son, don't think I wasn't just as scared as you were. Anyone who isn't scared in a situation like that is just a plain damn fool."

Grant # 1 - 7

Q: You could see the bombs coming at you?

Grant: Yes. You could see them leave the plane and head for us. By the time the bomb was half way down you could usually tell whether they were going to hit or not. Some of them came quite close and they splashed a lot of dirty and muddy water on us, and a few bomb fragments. They blew off our aerial so we had no communications until we got it fixed about two or three hours later.

Q: What were your reactions during the time of the attack?

Grant: I don't know. Just to zig and zag and try to miss the bombs.

Q: I've heard men say that they were so busy doing the job they had to do that they weren't aware of personal feelings or emotions.

Grant: That's true. I don't remember what my emotions really were but I must have been scared because anyone in a situation like that certainly is scared. Those people are shooting at him.
That brings to mind another little incident as told to me by a friend of mine: "Later on we'd been ordered to pick up the survivors of a troop ship which we had sunk. Several ships had gotten there before us and picked up most of the survivors, but we found one man swimming around still in the water. He was a black man and had been in the Army for

years and years. We picked him up and brought him aboard and either the next day or later on the same day, we had a shooting match with a couple of enemy destroyers. While they were shooting at us, of course, we were all at general quarters and everybody who didn't have something to do top side was down below. This one man whom we had picked up, was just standing up there in the fo'c'sle looking around and seemed to be enjoying things. I called to him to get below but he didn't hear me. After everything was over I called him up and asked him what was the matter with him. Wasn't he scared? Didn't he know enough to get below? He said, "Well, Captain, I've been in the Army for a long time. In the Army the enemy shoot right at you. But in the Navy the enemy only shoot at the ship. I wasn't scared."

Q: I'm sure you were grateful that that immediate attack was over. Were you able to have any communications? Your communications equipment was knocked down, you said.

Grant: We had previously, just before the attack, we had gotten off a dispatch to Manila saying that we were under attack and that was the first indication Manila had had that the Japs were anywhere around. When our antenna was shot off, we had no more communications with them. We couldn't send them any more messages or receive any messages. They thought we had probably been sunk. About two hours later we managed to get an auxiliary antenna operating because we weren't attacked again and had a chance to work on our antenna. We finally got word up to Manila that we were all safe. In the meantime we had gone down to Zamboanga and I put the wounded men ashore in a Philippine hospital. We then received orders to proceed to Balikpapan, Borneo.

Q: From whom did those orders come?

Grant: From Manila.

Q: Manila, or Cavite, had not been struck yet?

Grant: At that time I think she had been but at the time we were bombed she had not been and she didn't even know the Japs were near. Our message was the first indication that the Japs were in the vicinity and it wasn't very close vicinity either because Zamboanga was about five or six hundred miles south of Manila.

Q: But they were still giving you orders at the time?

Grant: Yes, and before we got the orders to go to Balikpapan I rather foolishly and naively thought, well, I'd better go back to Manila because maybe they need some help, which turned out to be rather foolish. Everyone was evacuating Manila.

Q: Three of your planes were sunk and you had --

Grant # 1   - 10 -

Grant: We had three more planes in the air and we managed to get word to them beofre our radio was shot off, to not come back to us but to proceed to another sea plane tender whose position we knew to be two or three hundred miles away. She was the SWAN.

Incidentally, when they got to the SAWN -- the SAWN was a small sea plane tender and conditions there were pretty crowded because the SWAN already had three of her own planes, but it was the only place I knew where they could get food and lodging for the night. They probably slept on deck but the tropics are kind of warm so it didn't matter so much.

Q: I'd like to have you describe the route you took to the south and the incidents that occurred along the way. This is the beginning of a remarkable odyssey.

Grant: When we left Zamboanga with orders to go to Balikpapan, we got supplementary orders to stop at two of the southern Philippine Islands, at Tutu and Tawitawi, and pick up two cruiser based planes which, for some reason or other, could not get back to their cruiser. We landed in either Tutu or Tawitawi and the planes were there sitting on the water. I believe they had been there all night by the time we arrived. We picked the crew up and towed one plane and hoisted another plane aboard and proceeded to Balik-papan. Balikpapan is on the northeast coast of Borneo. When we got there (we had been there about one day), we got orders to proceed south to Tarakan, which is also in Borneo. When we arrived there with no

Grant # 1 - 11 -

further incident, we found several U.S. ships which had previously evacuated Manila anchored there.

Q: How long did it take you to go from the Philippines to Balikpapan?

Grant: Just one day.

Q: What did your planes do?

Grant: The SWAN was still taking care of our planes. We were all by ourselves ~~and just evacuating the Philippines~~.

Q: How long did it take you to go from Balikpapan down to Tarakan?

Grant: About another day. It's not very far. There we came across many U.S. ships which had previously evacuated Manila. All the time we were there, which was three or four days, other ships would straggle in. Some of them *had been* shot up a little bit and others with no excitement to report.

Q: What did you do while you were in Tarakan?

Grant: We stayed there about three days. We refueled and then left with orders to go to Makassar. Makassar is in the southern Celebes, southwestern Celebes, where we were to refuel and await orders. We went down there as a fleet. There were about twenty ships, all together. I believe by that time all ships at Manila had evacuated. Most of the shore base commands had evacuated to Corregidor with General MacArthur and it was actually from Corregidor we were getting our orders, not from Manila.

Q: I wanted to clarify the armament which the PRESTON carried.

Grant: The PRESTON had its original two five-inch guns, which it had as a destroyer, one on the fo'c'sle and one on the fan tail. Our entire anti-aircraft armament consisted of only four fifty caliber guns which was as much as a PBY carried -- it was nothing. We didn't do much good against the planes which were attacking us.

We got orders about two o'clock one morning to leave Makassar and go to Darwin, Australia. We stopped at Soerabaja just about Christmas time. We went as a group -- the same group that left Tarakan. We spent Christmas day and Christmas Eve there. Soerabaja is on the eastern tip of Java right near Bali. I'm sorry to say we didn't have a chance to go over and see any interesting things at Bali.

Q: Did you meet any of the people in Soerabaja?

Grant: I looked up one or two wives of the Dutch officers whom I had previously met at Balikpapan and Tarakan, and they had asked me if I ever got to Soerabaja to please look them up and say hello for them, which I did.

Grant # 1 - 13 -

Q: Were you able to evaluate the feeling of the people toward the Dutch as opposed to the Japanese?

Grant: Everybody was in favor of the Dutch. Of course, there were mostly Dutch people whom I met there. I did not meet any natives. They were all afraid of the Japanese and were very glad to see us arrive, and sorry to see us leave in a few days. We arrived there with three sea plane tenders, all together -- the PRESTON, the SWAN, and the CHILDS. We had originally left Manila with a total of twenty-nine PBYs. By the time we got down there, we had probably only fifteen of the original twenty-nine PBYs left so we picked up a few more that the Dutch Navy had in Soerabaja and proceeded south with them. We went directly to Darwin and stayed there quite a while.

Q: Can you describe Darwin to me at the time you arrived?

Grant: Darwin was rather a small northern Australian town. I'd say the population was somehwere around ten or twelve thousand. There was desert country all around and it had nothing in the way of industry except a small meat packing plant. The people were very friendly. There was an Australian Air Force field there which sent out patrols to augment ours and were sort of standing by to assist our planes in case we needed help in our patrols. We kept patrolling the northern Australian coast, the Indian Ocean coast, and up as far as Java, and around New Guinea, and even Sumatra and the Celebes.

Q: Could your planes go that far?

Grant: Oh yes. We had rather a long range. While we were there, instead of operating entirely from Darwin, we would be sent back up north to about a hundred miles south of where the Japs had taken over. We'd anchor in some little bay or inlet in one of the small Celebes Islands and operate our planes from there. Very often we'd send out planes in the morning, three planes, for instance, and maybe two, or one, or none would come back. They'd be shot down by the Japanese.

All the natives in that area were very friendly toward the Americans. They didn't like the Japanese. When one of our planes got shot down, it would head for the nearest land on the way down (there were many islands around there) and land as close as they could to land and then swim ashore, those who could. Incidently, we lost very few pilots or crew members. They'd swim ashore; the natives were very good to them. They'd feed them and put them up for two or three days and even though we'd change our base of operations from one island to another every two or three days, the natives knew by some system of communication they had -- their drums -- just where we were. They'd pack up our crew in a canoe and send them back to us.

Q: Did you ever discover what their communication system was?

Grant: No, I never did but they always seemed to know. Sometimes three or four or five days after a plane was shot down, with no communication from the crew at all, a canoe would appear around the corner of the bay where we were and there would be the crew. And we would have shifted base in the meantime. In one instance it was almost three weeks before we heard from one crew and in accordance with Navy regulations, when a man is missing and considered dead, we are to sell all his personal possessions at auction and to send the proceeds back to his nearest kin. This one crew had been missing about three weeks, so we carried out regulations, sold all their possesions, and sent the money to the next of kin. The next day they showed up via the canoe route and were quite upset to find they didn't have any clothes left. Needless to say, the crew members who had bought their clothes were very happy to give them back.

Q: Were the people in Darwin friendly? Were they glad to see the Americans there?

Grant: Very friendly and glad to see the Americans.

Q: Were they fearful of the Japanese coming?

Grant: Oh yes. Everybody was everywhere. They were very glad that we had these patrols out to give them warning of what was coming. As I mentioned, we would go out to various places, various islands in the north, Probably the most interesting trip we had away from Darwin was to the Spice Islands at Ambon in the Celebes. We stayed there for just two or three days and then went over to a place called Kendari, which is on the southeastern tip of the Celebes. It was a very small bay and we knew the Japs were about a hundred miles north. There was very little maneuvering in this bay but it was very good sheltered anchorage for the planes. After we had put out the three buoys for our planes, I looked around for a place for an escape route. I noticed a rather high cliff, about twenty or thirty feet high, near the entrance to the bay, with a lot of palm trees growing on the top of it. After taking several soundings around the base of the cliff, I saw the water was deep enough so I could bring my ship right alongside. So I did. We tied up to these palm trees and I sent the crew ashore with knives and machetes and axes to chop down all the greenery they could find. They brought them back aboard ship and we completely camouflaged the ship from stem to stern and up in the stacks. The boys must have made a pretty good job because later that afternoon, some Japanese fighter planes showed up. Our planes, in the meantime, had gone out on patrol, so there were no planes in the bay. The Japanese saw the buoys in the bay -- they came down low over them and spotted them and some of them flew over us at less than a hundred feet but they didn't see us. We, of course, were at general quarters and I had some trigger happy boys on there who wanted to shoot but I gave orders not to shoot unless we were fired at because I thought maybe they wouldn't see us. And luckily they didn't. Our boys had done a good job of camouflaging. During the attack three of our planes were returning. I saw them coming back over the horizon. I opened up on the radio in plain English and told them to stay clear because we were under attack. Usually you communicate with your planes by code but there was no time for that. I was very relieved when I saw them turn around and disappear and luckily the Japs hadn't seen them. When the attack was over, I told them to come on in. They came in and landed, this was late afternoon, and the next morning they took off and we also took off, heading south.

Q: Could you feel a surge of relief through the whole crew after this attack had passed?

Grant: Oh yes. Any commanding officer or executive officer can feel how the crew feels just by the way they act. Of course there was a surge of relief but we didn't know how soon they'd be back again. They knew the buoys were there so they must have known there was some action going on.

Q: What was the complement of the PRESTON?

Grant: I believe there was about a hundred and twenty-five. Each plane had about eight crew members so in addition to the hundred and twenty-five we had about, usually aboard, three or four plane crews. There were about eight or ten officers.

Q: Was your logistics problem of getting provisions and ammunition a serious one?

Grant # 1 - 18

Grant: Oh yes. We had to watch out for that all the time. Every time we'd go back to Darwin, of course, we'd fill up again on everything we could possibly hold. We'd also buy chickens, vegetables, etc., from the natives of the various islands.

Q: Were they able to give you the things you needed?

Grant: At Darwin, yes. There were several supply ships in there. At the shore establishment we could get gasoline and oil from the Australians in Darwin. No problem. They were very happy to give it to us, very happy to help us.

Q: Was there just the one military installation there at Darwin?

Grant: As far as I remember there was just this one Australian Air Force base. There were, in addition, a few small Army anti-aircraft units.

Q: What were the port facilities?

Grant: They had only one dock and there was rather a large anchorage. There were probably as many as fifty ships in there. For a small Australian town, they did have rather good port facilities.

Q: Were you still receiving operation orders from a higher command?

Grant: Yes. I'm not sure when the command shifted from Corregidor

Grant #1 - 19 -

down to the fleet we were in. On several occasions when we left for various bases and various islands, we had been given orders to do this and that, which we carried out to the best of our ability, but sometimes the situation would change so rapidly that it wasn't feasible, or it wasn't the best thing to do, to carry out those orders explicitly. I had to waste a lot of time sending back a dispatch saying "In view of this or that, I request permission to do thus and so." I finally hit upon the idea of sending a dispatch saying, "Unless I hear otherwise, I'm going to do thus and so." That worked fine because not once did I ever receive a dispatch saying not to do that. I talked with members of the staff later and they told me that they were always glad to receive a dispatch like that from me because they wouldn't have to call a staff meeting and discuss whether I should do it or not. They'd just sit back and say, "If Grant goofs this one, we'll give him Hell."

Q: I would think they couldn't possibly have been as aware of the tactical situation from where they were.

Grant: No. They couldn't anticipate all contingencies. Several of them came up very rapidly and very hurriedly and we just had to change our standing orders.

Q: Did you feel that you were able to accomplish anything?

Grant: Once in a while we were able to spot some Jap planes or

Grant # 1 - 20

a few ships and radio back to headquarters, wherever that happened to be, that we had seen such and such a plane or such and such a ship. We didn't dare get too close to them because we had no protective armament at all on the planes except a few fifty caliber guns.

Q: When you left Kendari after the camouflag had worked so successfully, did you go directly back to Darwin?

Grant: No, we stopped at Buton, which was probably a hundred miles or so south of Kendari. We conducted patrols from there and stayed there four or five days all together. It was the longest we had stayed in one place for a long time.

Q: Why did you stay for so long?

Grant: Because the Japanese had not made any forays farther south for those several days and we thought we might as well stay there -- at least the admiral thought we might as well because there was no danger of our getting over-run at the time, so we stayed as long as we could. The admiral at that time was in the fleet, which I believe was stationed in Darwin.

Q: How much control was exerted over operations? Or could you almost operate on your own?

Grant: We were on what's called independent duty but we still had to report to the boss. Everybody in the Navy has a boss, even the Chief of Naval Operations. The present CNO, incidentally, happened to be a lieutenant on my ship at that time. He was in one of the squadrons on the ship. He now is chairman of Joint Chiefs of Staff, Tommy Moorer. I think I made a pretty good job in bringing him up.

We stayed at Buton for four or five days and I paid my usual courtesy call on the governor there. The governor was a Dutchman, of course, who had been in the islands for probably twenty years or so, and he knew the natives very well and was very sympathetic to their points of view. He did not like some of the orders which he would get from the Dutch. One in particular he told me that was very misunderstood by the natives. They couldn't understand what the order was all about. That was a simple little order to the effect that in the future all women in public should cover their breasts. Usually, up until then, they would walk around with just a sarong on and nothing else. But when this order came out, it puzzled them, and they couldn't understand it anymore than probably someone in the Mohammedan countries where the women would have to cover her nose and mouth. But it was the law so whenever they would come to town, most of them would put on sort of bikini bras, but some of them wouldn't. The governor said, "Come with me. I want to show you what I mean." So we went out to the streets and walked around the block. Most of the women, as I say, had a bikini-type bra on but once in a while we'd see a woman in the distance without one. She'd see the governor coming and know that she had to make everything legal so she picked up her sarong and covered her breasts. Of course, we could see everything else but there was nothing illegal about that. He said, "You see what I mean?"

Q: What type of village was Buton?

Grant: Very small, three or four thousand people maybe. There may have been twenty or thirty Dutch, the rest of them were all natives.

Q: When you were so far away from your usual operation area, did you have the feeling you were deserted or away from contact of what was going on?

Grant: No. I never had that feeling at all because we were always so busy. A person feels deserted, I believe, only when he's lonely and can't find something to do. That was one of the least of my problems. There was always something to do. We were right in the middle of the war --we had to be on lookout twenty-four hours a day.

Q: Of course, Darwin being right on the north coast was closer to it than the people who were around in Fremantle and Perth.

Grant: Yes. The people down there were not very worried. Although I happened to be, about six months later, in Sydney the day those six small submarines came in and shot up the place. From Buton we came back to Darwin. In the meantime we had taken off most of our camouflage but there were still a few palm fronds stuck up in the top of the ship's antenna and the stacks, and everybody sort of looked at us askance when we appeared at Darwin. The first thing I did when we got to Darwin, late in the evening, was to make plans to go ashore the next day and make arrangements for re-supplying the ship. Needless to say, we were very short on fuel, very short on food, and short on general supplies, including clothes for men. So early the next morning, I left the ship in command of my executive officer and went ashore. We had about six planes at that time anchored close by --three of them had gone on patrol but there were three left. While I was ashore, at the American consul's office, trying to make arrangements to get the ship reprovisioned, we heard some sirens going off. We all ran out to see what was going on and up in the air about twenty thousand feet, we saw two squadrons of Japanese planes coming in. They were quite high and the few anti-aircraft guns that the Australians were able to muster did not have enough power to even get up there. In a few minutes the one squadron broke off, came down, and they turned out to be dive bombers. They attacked all the ships in the harbor. There must have been thirty or forty of them in the harbor at the time. They strafed them and bombed them and a few of the planes were shot down, but not very many.

In the meantime, the other group of planes remained at their high altitude and started dropping bombs on the ships that were left at anchor and also started dropping bombs on the town in general. We got in some slit trenches and waited until the attack was over. After the planes had left, presumably going back to their carriers for refueling, I made my way back to the dock and attempted to get back to my ship. When I arrived at the dock, my boat, in which I had come ashore, was no where in sight. After wandering around for a while I came across three or four Australians who were rather anxious to do something to help although they didn't know exactly what to do. There were several ships sinking in the harbor which had been previously hit -- some of them were still under way. I noticed my own ship which was underway but smoking rather badly from the stern. I could tell from the way it was maneuvering it was in trouble. I found out later it had the rudder shot off and one engine out of commission.

Q: How many bombs had hit it?

Grant: I didn't know at that time, but later --there was one bomb which had hit astern right in the ammunition rack and had blown up all our ready ammunition on deck and killed about ten percent of the crew. It was just one bomb which had done the damage.

There was one boat drawn up on the beach and these Australians and I took this one boat out with the idea of picking up survivors of one American destroyer which was about a half a mile from shore, which was sinking. It's bow was up in the air and it was disappearing under water. We took the boat out to try to rescue some of the men who were swimming around from this destroyer. There had been one ammunition ship which was tied up to the only dock there, and that ammunition ship had been hit and was burning in three or four places. It had been hit by more than one bomb. On our way out to rescue these men, the bow of the ammunition ship blew up when we were only about two hundred yards from her. The next thing I knew, I was in the water swimming around.

Q: Was the water on fire?

Grant: Not at the moment. I looked around and looked up and saw a lot of hot burning debris up there which had been blown up from the ammunition ship, falling down on me. I figured that the deeper I could dive under water, the colder these hot metals would be when they hit me. So I took a deep breath and dove down as long as I could. I came up for a breath and saw the stuff still falling down and dove again. I could hear this hissing metal hit the water. Luckily, I was not hit at all, very luckily. When I came up for the third time, all the debris had settled. I saw that I was drifting down on the ammunition ship. The ammunition ship had also, when it blew up, spewed a lot of oil in the water and the oil was burning and I was going right down on this burning oil. Luckily, I drifted by a buoy, a rather large ship's buoy, and it had about a ten or twenty foot line trailing from it. I swam over to it and was able to grab ahold of the line and hauled myself hand over hand back to the buoy before I got caught in the burning oil. There was rather a strong tide in Darwin and even though the oil was spreading rather rapidly, the tide kept it away from me and kept it going down tide. I tried to climb up on top of the buoy but the buoy had too high a freeboard and I couldn't make it. It was quite slick and I just hung onto the line, but my weight and the tide made me sort of weather cocked down toward the ammunition ship. I was on the ammunition ship's side of the buoy. Everyonce in a while, one or two more shells would go off in the ammunition ship. I thought it would be the better part of valor if I could get around to the other side of the buoy so I managed to do that, hand over hand, grabbing a hold of a few bolts and protrudences [PROTUBERANCES] on the buoy. It was quite a job. I had taken my shoes off but I still had my shirt and my short trousers. We were in tropical dress then.

Q: Was it cold?

Grant: No the water was quite warm.

Q: But you had to hang on to the line with one hand while you were trying to manuever with your feet and the other hand.

Grant: That's right. I didn't dare let go with that one line because I'd be gone.

Q: How high was the buoy above your head?

Grant: The top of the buoy was probably three feet above the water and I couldn't get a hold of it to pull myself up on top of the buoy. I just pulled myself around to the other side and finally by sort of half swimming and half dog paddling I kept up ship from the buoy.

In the meantime one or two small boats would go by trying to rescue the original people that I had set out to rescue. I was so close to the ammunition ship and I knew it was dangerous to have anyone get that close so I didn't call them. I knew I was safe and I didn't want them to come in and maybe get blown up by something, so I just let them go on by and I stayed there until it was all over. There were a lot of sharks in Darwin harbor --it's famous for sharks. But I guess the sharks were as scared as I was, and luckily I didn't think about the sharks until I got ashore --I had too many other things to think about.

Q: Did you tie the line around your waist?

Grant # 1 - 28

Grant: Yes, I did when I was trying to get up there. About that time (This was about noon and I had been in the water about noon and I had been in the water about an hour and a half) the bombers had returned from their carrier, refueled and rebombed, and came back for a second attack. This attack was aimed mostly at the Australian air field but they still let loose a few bombs on the ships in the harbor. Some of those bombs fell rather close to me. I found out that certain private parts of my anatomy were rather subject to shock, the concussion. So whenever I'd see a bomb heading in my direction, I'd pull myself as far out of the water as I could.

After that attack was over the tide had slackened enough so that I could swim ashore. Not only did I want to get to shore, but the burning oil at that time, now that the tide had slackened, was coming up towards me, so I thought I'd better get out of there. I swam to the nearest dock, about a quarter mile away. This was not a dock but just a small pier: there was only one dock to which the ammunition ship was tied. I was so tired that I couldn't pull myself up on the pier, so I hung on until some men came out and helped me up. Just about that time a couple of shells blew up on the ammunition ship. One of them made a direct hit on the buoy I had been hanging to and I saw it slowly sink. Lucky Grant, again!

Q: You must have been in quite good physical condition in any case because you were almost forty years old then, weren't you?

Grant: Just about. But I had always been a good swimmer. I could swim a couple of miles with no trouble, so the swimming part didn't bother me at all. I wasn't the slightest bit afraid or worried about water. It was just hanging on and even though the water was fairly warm, I got cold and I started to shiver in the water. The water was probably in the seventies, *or eighties* but being in the water so long, I was cold. I don't remember being really frightened because I knew I could take care of myself. It's only when I can't take care of myself that I'm frightened. I suppose that's more or less natural. If you don't know what's happening and if you think you can't take care of yourself, then you are frightened. If you know you can take care of yourself, it doesn't do any good to be frightened.

Q: So some people did help you up on the dock?

Grant: Yes. I walked to shore. There were still some dead bodies lying around and I didn't have any shoes on and I'm not ashamed to say that I "borrowed" a pair of shoes from one of the bodies.

Q: Were the people who had been killed civilians, military, or both?

Grant: Both. When I got my shoes I made my way back to the consulate's office and when I got there, about half of it had been bombed. It was not burning but it was sort of wrecked and there was nobody there. I found a note attached to one of the desks addressed to me saying they had all evacuated and if I should survive and come back, please take charge.

Grant #1 - 30 -

Q: Who left you the note?

Grant: The consulate.

Q: What type of building was it?

Grant: Just a small wooden building with a few bedrooms attached to it.

Q: Was his office on the first floor?

Grant: Yes, it was on the first floor. There was a second floor with bedrooms and living quarters up there.

Q: What was the weather like that day?

Grant: The weather was fine --you could see for miles, sunshine. No smog. This was in February --February 19.

Q: How much damage was done to the military and the town besides the ships?

Grant: Most of the damage to the town itself was down by the wharfs. I don't think the Japanese really tried to bomb the civilian homes --just a few stray bombs happened to land there-- but they were concentrating mainly on the shore installations, and the ships.

Grant # 1 - 31 -

Q: Was this the first attack?

Grant: The first and only attack on Darwin. Of course, everybody was afraid that after the attack the Japs would stage a landing attack. Everybody was quite worried. That was the main reason why the consul had left and thousands of other people had left and headed south towards Alice Springs.

Q: How did they go?

Grant: By car, jeep. There was a train there but I think the train had gone. There were no regular schedules at that time. I think the only train there probably left with standing room only.

Q: How much intelligence information were you able to receive?

Grant: None whatsoever. It was entirely a surprise attack. No intelligence on the landings at all. We didn't know they were coming, we didn't have any warning to leave but it seemed the better part of valor on the part of the consulate to leave.

Q: What did the PRESTON do when she was hit?

Grant: When I was hanging onto the buoy, I saw her leaving the harbor and although I was congratulating Les Wood who was my exec,

Grant #1 - 32 -

on doing a fine job of handling her with a broken rudder and one engine out, it did give me sort of a lonely feeling to be hanging onto this buoy and see my ship go out.

Q: So you went back and became consul?

Grant: One might say that but when I got word to take charge, I didn't know what to take charge of. While I was wondering what to take charge of, some of our boys who had been in the planes that had been shot up had made their way ashore and asked their way to the consul's office. When they got there, they were quite surprised to find that I was the consul.

Q: Had you gotten any dry clothes by then?

Grant: No, it was a nice warm day and they dried pretty well by then.

Q: What was your grade then?

Grant: Lieutenant Commander. I stayed there about three days. I didn't ever receive any word from the consul --where he was or anything. I was finally able to get word down to our naval headquarters, which was then in Perth, that I was there with several of my men, and requested they send a plane up to pick me up.

Grant # 1 - 33 -

Q: What communications did you use?

Grant: I used the Australian military communications system which was still operating. I got word down and they sent a plane up for us. They knew where the PRESTON was. The PRESTON had gone down about five or six hundred miles and was anchored in a small bay near a place called Darby. She had gone west and south. There I picked up the ship and we proceeded south -- about ten knots was all we could make -- to Fremantle.

Q: What was the attitude aboard ship of this severe loss of life?

Grant: They took it in their stride. The dead had been all buried at sea before I got aboard. There were a few wounded, but not very many. Everybody had either been killed or just slightly wounded. There was no one whom we had to put ashore in a hospital when we got down to Fremantle. At Fremantle (probably a thousand miles or so) they gave us temporary repairs.

Q: Did you go independently?

Grant: Independently until we got to Fremantle. That took four or five days. We were low on oil and provisions by the time we got down there. From my experience in Darwin, I did not go into Fremantle harbor. I anchored outside. We had only one anchor left because I had lost one already in Zamboanga. But I did not go in this very small and narrow harbor; I anchored outside

Grant # 1 - 34 -

just in case the Japs would come around again and I could get out of there.

I went in by boat and made arrangements to have temporary repairs and then, of course, I had to take my ship in, which I did just long enough for repairs and then got out again.

Q: What repairs were they able to make in Fremantle?

Grant: There was a large hole in the deck which they planked over and they were able to stop the leak in one of our stern tubes, which had made us have the pumps running constantly --it was rather a bad leak. After we had temporary repairs, which didn't increase our speed any, we got orders to go to Sydney for permanent repairs. The Australians had a dry dock there. So again, at ten knots, we went all the way around the southern part of Australia --it must have been twenty-five hundred miles-- up to Sydney.

Q: What was the trip like?

Grant: It was good weather except for about a week we had about a thirty or forty knot wind blowing directly from the south. It was a little cold and having blown for such a long time from this one direction, south, the swells became exceedingly high. As best we could (we measured them with a sexton when we were down at the bottom of them) measure, the swells were about eighty feet high, but we rode it just like a rocking chair. We were short compared with the swells, probably a quarter of a mile between the crest of each swell and we just rode it very gently, no trouble at all.

Q: Was it a frightening experience?

Grant: No, not at all because it was so easy. The thirty knot wind just kicked up a few waves on top of the swells. There was nothing frightening about that at all. It probably took us about a week or ten days. When we finally got to Sydney, we went into dry dock there and they made a very good job of repairing us. In addition to the actual repair work on the damage that was done, I inveigled a few extra guns out of the Australians which we certainly needed badly. They were twenty millimeters instead of our fifty caliber. In the meantime, incidentally, whenever we had lost a plane, or a plane was beached, I would send a boat ashore and take all the fifty caliber guns from the plane --the plane itself was of no use. By the time we got to Darwin, instead of our original four fifty caliber guns, we must have had thirty or forty, which we had rescued from the planes.

Q: Were you able to mount them?

Grant: We mounted them on stanchions around the railing. That's the only thing we rescued from the planes. They all worked fine and we had plenty of ammunition.

Grant # 1 - 36 -

Q: In Sydney the workmen were civilian?

Grant: No, it was an Australian navy dry dock. They were very good and they were very happy to work on us. It took about two months to have us completely repaired. We left the dry dock and were anchored in Sydney Bay for about three or four days before we left there and went back to Perth.

Q: What were the activities of the crew in those two months?

Grant: Leave, liberty and recreation, except they helped the Australians during the day with repairs. Several of our boys fell in love with, and a couple of them married, Australian girls there in Sydney. Later on one or two of them did in Perth and Fremantle. After we left the dry dock in Sydney, we were three or four days in the harbor there provisioning and getting ready to leave for Fremantle.

One evening about eight o'clock at night, the general alarm went off in the harbor, and it turned out to be four Japanese midget submarines which had gotten through the nets and come in and were firing torpedoes. The submarines were probably not more than thirty feet long, a one man submarine, with one torpedo and one small periscope. All the ships in the harbor were shooting at anything that went by that looked like a submarine. Some of the gunners on my ship opened up at something they thought was a periscope and it turned out to be the handle of a swab. But the shells were bouncing all over the place that night. One or two ships were hit by torpedoes. One torpedo went right underneath the USS CHICAGO, which was tied up at one of the docks. It went under the CHICAGO and hit the dock and blew up but the CHICAGO wasn't hurt. No ship was hurt except superficially.

Q: Were they kamikaze submarines?

Grant: Yes.

Q: They didn't expect to get out?

Grant: No. Although the Australians thought four of them came in, I don't know why they thought there were four, but they did capture or sink three of them. The fourth one they never did find.

Q: Were any submariners captured?

Grant: No, they were all killed. As you say, it was a kamikaze raid. Speaking of kamikaze, at one time we were under kamikaze attack when we were anchored at night in a small lagoon with a fleet -- there must have been about twenty of our ships in there. And when the alarm went off, of course, all ships darkened ship. On one of the islands there was a radio mast with a red light on it. This kamikaze plane came in right over us about two hundred feet and went right into the base of this tower thinking it was a ship. The next morning, we went over there and there were two bodies in this kamikaze airplane. We could never figure out why two of them. The other one couldn't have been coming along to learn how to do it. This was at Ulithi two or three years later.

We left Sydney and returned to Perth. About a month or two later, I got a dispatch from the Chief of Naval Operations, signed "Ensign Jones by direction of Chief of Naval Operations," calling my attention to one article in the Navy regulations which says, in effect, that when a commanding officer takes his ship to a foreign port for repairs, unless he has previously received permission from the Chief of Naval Operations, he, the commanding officer, is personally responsible for the bill for the cost of repairs. It came addressed directly to me as commanding officer who was personally responsible for the cost of repairs. Well, if the cost of repairs had been five or six thousand dollars, I might have been a little bit worried, but the cost of repairs was a half a million so I wasn't the slightest bit worried.

Q: What answer did you make to the letter?

Grant: I didn't make any answer at all.

Q: You probably found in war time it was easier to operate than with the bureaucratic red tape of peace time.

Grant: Much easier.

Grant #1 - 39 -

Q: Was the PRESTON then in good shape?

Grant: The PRESTON was in very good shape. We were back to twenty-five knots and had about six twenty millimeter guns, I believe, in addition to all the fifty calibers which we still carried. We never had to use any of them after that. We kept operating on the west coast of Australia for about a year.

Q: Was your crew replaced?

Grant: No. Just a few replacements --just the regular people who had been aboard and had been away from home for three years were sent back and we got replacements for them.

Q: How many PBYs did you have?

Grant: We had about six, our full complement.

Q: Were you based in Fremantle?

Grant: There was another four stacker converted into a sea plane tender with whom we swapped duties. Fremantle was sort of a rest and recreation port. Our main base for reconnaissance patrols was about five or six hundred miles north in a place called Exmouth Gulf, north of Shark's Bay. We operated out of there and took turns with this other ship, the CHILDS. The commanding officer of the

CHILDS was a classmate of mine. We'd each go up there for about two or three weeks and then come back to Fremantle for a week or ten days rest, liberty, and recreation.

Q: When you were operating, how far would the ship go out before the planes would start to patrol?

Grant: We wouldn't patrol until we got all the way out to Exmouth Gulf. In the meantime the ship that was at the bay would continue to patrol until we got there and relieved them. The planes would rotate, too.

Q: How far could the planes patrol?

Grant: They could patrol a thousand miles or so. We patrolled the north and west coast of Australia up toward Java, Sumatra and New Guinea.

Q: Did you have any incidents with the Japs during that time?

Grant: No. We'd spot a few of them but nothing that really amounted to anything. After their first attack on Darwin, they didn't make any attempt to land at all. They made one other attack on Darwin several months later and one other attack a little farther south at, I believe, Carnarvon, but it was very sporadic and really didn't amount to anything.

I wanted to mention more about Tommy Moorer. This happened to

Grant #1 - 41 -

be the morning of the attack at Darwin which I have previously mentioned. Whenever the planes would take off on their patrol, they'd leave at daybreak, sometimes at four o'clock in the morning. I made it a point always to be up at the gangway to see the boys off. When Tommy left the ship that morning, he saluted and said, "Well, goodbye, Captain. I don't think I'll see you tonight." I said, "Tommy what are you talking about?" He said, "I sort of feel I won't see you tonight." I said, "Tommy, don't be silly, of course you will. We'll be greeting you as we always do."

Well, it seem that before the Japs came in to attack Darwin, they shot his plane down and he landed on the water. He and his radioman were in a life raft alone (I think the other members of the crew had gotten killed or drowned), and a Dutch tanker came along. They waved frantically and the Dutch tanker saw them and picked them up. About an hour or two later, the Dutch tanker got sunk by Japanese planes, so Tommy and the radioman got out their raft and paddled around again. They finally went ashore on some little island through the reef.

In the meantime we had sent planes out looking for them. They happened to be land planes and they went near this island and saw these two men waving. We figured there's the crew of the plane that got shot down. We sent a mine sweeper out that afternoon or the next morning but the reef was so close to the shore they couldn't get through. They stayed outside the reef and sent a signal in by flashlight and told Tommy and his radioman to take the raft out beyond the reef and they would pick them up then. (This was daytime). When they got out just beyond the reef, a Jap plane came along, and sank the minesweeper so they had to go back to the island. The next day we sent a seaplane out there and picked them up. Tommy was certainly right -- "I won't see you tonight, Captain." That was the day the Japs came over and bombed up Darwin. I didn't see Tommy for three or four months.

The Australians and the American got along quite well there in Fremantle but naturally there was a certain amount of rivalry between us. I remember one morning I was holding mast and there were two boys who came up that had been arrested by the shore patrol the night before for being drunk and disorderly. I asked them what the story was. They sort of looked at each other and one of them spoke up and said, "Well, Sir, Captain, we was just walking along the sidewalk doing nothing, it was a narrow sidewalk and there were four Aussies coming down toward us. We wasn't going to get off into the gutter for any Aussie so we stopped and they stopped. None of us said anything for awhile and then one of the Aussies said, 'Well, there's four of us and two of you, you'd better get off the sidewalk and let us by.' My boy said, 'No, we're not going to do that.' So the Aussie said, 'Well, the only thing to do is have a fight and see what happens.' My boy spoke up and said, 'Gee, that's certainly fair, isn't it? Four against two.' The Aussie said, 'Well, Mate, you don't understand. We'll toss up and see who loses. The one of us who loses will go on your side and there'll be three against three. We'll have a big fight and whoever wins, the other will get off the sidewalk.'

Well, they had a big fight and when it was over they put their arms around each other, went into the nearest pub and got drunk. Afterwards they became pretty good friends. In fact, one of my boys married the sister of one of the Aussies.

Q: Why were they at mast then? Had the shore patrol picked them up?

Grant: Yes, they had gotten drunk in the pub. It wasn't the fight, it was getting drunk in the pub.

Q: You told me that toward the end of your duty in western Australia, you acted in the capacity of almost a counter spy. Can you tell me what that was?

Grant: After I got relieved of command of the PRESTON, the admiral asked me if I wanted to go home right away. So I said, "Sure." He said, "Well, I have a job coming up which might interest you. We know that there are Japanese coast watchers up on the northwest coast of Australia and we'd like someone to sort of check them out and we'd also like to find out where might be a good base for sea planes in addition to the one one that you have at North West Cape." I said, "All right, I'll take that job, too." He said, "Well, it's a little different from most of your jobs, I think. You'll have to be disguised as a pearl fisherman, Australian pearl fisherman, and go up there in sixty foot water and have as your executive officer, your assistant, a man who has been a pearler and knows the country very well." I said, "I hardly would have accepted the job unless I had someone with me who knew the coast." The first thing I did was to look up the charts of the coast and I found out the latest chart had written down in the lower right hand corner, in parenthesis, "corrected 1902" so I knew that they didn't know much about that coast.

I was flown up to Broome, Australia, and there I met the man who was to be my exec, who was really the skipper of the ship, as far as I was concerned. I considered him the skipper. He knew how to handle those luggers and I didn't. In addition we had a crew of about six native Australians. We started from Broome and went on up to a place called Derby and then from there, we were on our own. We put in at various little bays and inlets and asked the natives if there had been any signs of Japanese activity around there. Very seldom would we find any of the natives who spoke English. They all spoke their own native language except once in awhile we'd land near a place where there happened to be a missionary. A lot of the natives used to work for the missionaries. They would always refer to it as working for "Mr. God." They would hoe his potato patch or get his breakfast, or something like that and they could speak a fair amount of English.

One place we went to, incidentally, there was a native who spoke very good English and we asked him where he learned English. He said, "Oh, I learn English down in Fremantle." We said,

"What were you doing in Fremantle?" He said, "Oh, one time many years ago, there was a bad man in my tribe, a very bad man, so I killed him. You people from Fremantle send someone up here to find out about it and they find out that the relatives of this man I killed are very mad at me. They want to kill me back. So you take me back to Fremantle and you save me. You put me in a great big house with a small room and you put bars on the outside of the room so the relatives cannot come and get me." He had no idea that he had been put in jail for killing this man. We were protecting him, and that's where he learned his English. He said, "They kept me there for two years and then they find out that maybe the relatives forget about it so they let me go and sent me back." He had no idea he was in jail. He thought we were protecting him.

Q: So he was friendly?

Grant: Very friendly.

We looked around for various hiding places of the Japanese coast watchers and we found two or three of them from the "grape vine" system of the natives, but never did we find anyone there. We found fireplaces and sort of little huts, but never did we find one single Japanese and we went all along that coast for about six weeks.

Q: How wide an area did you cover?

Grant: It was from Exmouth Gulf up to Wyndham, which is a little southwest of Darwin. Probably five or six hundred miles. And we never did find any of the Japanese although we did find indications of their having been there. It was a very interesting trip and I enjoyed it very much. A plane flew up to get me and brought me back again and the Australian lieutenant brought the ship back.

Q: How did you handle your operation? Did you stay in some little bay at night and then start out the next morning?

Grant: Yes, and sometimes we'd stay in that bay for three or four days looking around, and go back up in the hills a little bit if there happened to be hills close to the shore. If the hills were way back, we wouldn't bother about it because we knew the Japs wouldn't be way back in the hills. But if the hills were close to the shore where they could watch and see the ships go by, then we would investigate. We always carried guns, of course, just in case, but the Japs had always left.

Q: Do you think they knew you were coming?

Grant: They must have through the grape vine. All natives seem to have grape vines and we don't know how they operate, but they seem to work.

Q: I don't picture the Japanese as being friendly with the natives.

Grant # 1 - 47 -

Grant: They weren't but the natives knew that the Japanese were up there and they'd tell them perhaps that "some boat come in now." They wouldn't say, "Get away." They'd just say some boat come in now and the Japs would figure, gee, maybe we'd better get out of here.

Q: How did you dress to be a pearl fisherman?

Grant: I dressed in short khaki shorts and open necked shirt. About two weeks before I left, I stained my face with walnut peels so I would get very, very tan and look as though I were a native pearl fisherman. It was a very interesting trip. In fact, it was almost as interesting as the first part of the war was. I enjoyed it very much and was sorry when it was over. I'm sorry we didn't find any Japanese. Maybe if we had I wouldn't be here talking to you.

Q: You spoke of growing a beard. Did you do that before you started this duty or while you were performing it?

Grant: When I heard I was going to get this duty, which was about two weeks previous to my going on duty, I grew a beard while I was still staining my face with the walnut juice. Actually it turned into a not very bad beard. My wife said I looked like Christ from my picture.

Grant # 1 - 48 -

Q: When you finished this duty, that concluded your tour in the western Pacific and you returned to the United States.

Grant: That's right. Then I had some shore duty in the Pentagon, which is always rather boring.

Q: You went from Australia to the naval air station in Jacksonville, didn't you?

Grant: That's right. I went to Jacksonville and was in command of the A and R, which I believe they now call ONR, and stayed there probably nine or ten months. Then I was sent to Tacoma, Washington to put in commission the CUMBERLAND SOUND which was a large new type sea plane tender. When that was commissioned, we were sent down to Long Beach for our indoctrination training.

When I first took command of the CUMBERLAND SOUND as prospective commanding officer, I believe thy call it, I first looked up the history of the officers who were going to serve on the ship and I found out to my consternation, that only one was a Naval Academy graduate, and only two out of the fifty had ever been to sea before. I thought to myself --my gosh, I have to take this ship out to sea!!

Q: In those days I guess that wasn't particularly unusual, was it?

Grant: No, probably not, but to me it was rather a traumatic experience because I had never had command of a ship with so few experienced officers. I knew there were several chief petty officers aboard who had been there for several years (in the Navy). On my first personnel inspection, I found out that there were about twenty chiefs with three and four hash marks on their arm, so I wasn't worried anymore about that ship. I knew chiefs that had been in the Navy for sixteen or twenty years could really handle things. Of course the senior chief, I made Chief Master at Arms and he did a very good job. I could still tell, as most commanding officers can, that something was wrong but I didn't really know what was wrong. So one day I called in the Chief Master at Arms, and old chief who had been in the Navy for twenty years, and asked him what was the matter with the ship, what was the matter with the men. He said, "Captain, you want me to tell you true?" I said, "I certainly do. That's what I called you in here for." He said, "Well Captain, these young kids --I mean Sir, I mean these young officers-- don't know anything about the Navy; they don't know anything about discipline; they call the men by their first name and they let the men call them by their first name, which, of course, is not very good for discipline. When some of the men do something wrong and I put them on report, their division officer gets them out of it. I am practically helpless. I certainly would appreciate it if something could be done about it."

I said, "Well, I certainly agree with you, Chief. I knew something was wrong but I didn't know what it was. What do you suggest?" He said, "Well, there has to be a little more discipline on here and if you will appoint me, if you will excuse the expression, Chief Son of a Bitch on this ship, I'll get things in order, if you'll back me up." I said, "Okay, Chief, from now on you're Chief Son of a Bitch; I'll back you up at every mast case there is." In about a month things were really straightened out. In the meantime, of course, I'd called in the officers and gave them a little lecture on what the Navy was all about, and what the difference was between Navy discipline and discipline in an office ashore, and they understood it. They were all nice kids, but they had never been to sea before and this was an entirely different view point which they had to assimilate and get used to.

Anyway when we went down to Long Beach for our indoctrination cruises, which lasted about three months, we got a citation from the training command down there to the effect that we were the best ship that had ever been trained for the last year. I gave credit for it all to my Chief Son of a Bitch.

Q: After you had been through the training command in Long Beach, what were the operations for the CUMBERLAND SOUND?

Grant: We first went out to Kwajalein. On the way we stopped at Hawaii and got the final orders from Admiral Nimitz and we went to Kwajalein. On the way I got orders from Admiral Nimitz explaining just what our program was going to be. We stayed in Kwajalein for maybe a month or so, sending out patrols all around the atoll. There must have been twenty or thirty U.S. ships in there. We were patrolling the whole atoll to be sure that no Japanese planes sneaked up on us.

Then, after the whole Navy moved a little farther west, we went to Ulithi, which is a large atoll southwest of Guam, not far from Yap. There we stayed for another three or four months, sending out patrols twenty-four hours a day around the whole atoll of Ulithi just to be sure that no Japanese planes came in and surprised us.

Q: How many planes did you have?

Grant: I think we had twelve planes at that time. It was on that occasion, when we were in Ulithi, that the kamikaze came over which I previously had mentioned.

When the war was practically at an end, we were ordered up to Tokyo Bay. We arrived there in the middle of a typhoon and had to steam around outside the bay two or three hundred miles away until the typhoon was over. Then we came back and I happened to be one of six ships which was ordered to Tokyo Bay three days before the peace treaty was signed. Our duties then were to establish a sea plane base and run logistic flights between Tokyo and Guam, bringing up all sorts of supplies which were needed in an emergency—things that ships could bring but it would take too long to bring. We had Also to patrol the entire coast of Japan to be sure that Japan was

Grant #1 - 52 -

living up to its committments in the peace treaty and not having any ships around which might threaten our ships.

Q: This is preparatory to the peace treaty signing?

Grant: Both preparatory to, and also after. The Japanese had surrendered but there had been no peace treaty signed. When Admiral Nimitz arrived from Hawaii, I happened to be the one who met him at his plane when he landed in Tokyo Bay from Hawaii.

Q: Where were you when you met him?

Grant: I was in Tokyo Bay. I had a small boat which I took out to his plane, met him, and took him immediately to the MISSOURI, where, as everyone knows, the peace treaty was signed.

Q: Can you tell me what he looked like, what he said, what his attitude was?

Grant: If you know Admiral Nimitz, he doesn't say very much at any time. I said, "Good afternoon, Admiral. This is quite an eventful day, isn't it?" He said, "Yeh." And I think that's all the conversation I had from there on all the way to the MISSOURI. I tried to say a few things making an effort to make him feel at home but he, as everyone knows, is very taciturn and doesn't say

Grant #1 - 53 -

very much, although I'm very fond of him and always have been. He's a very nice gentleman.

Q: Who was with him?

Grant: Some of his staff officers. We took him to the MISSOURI and it was the next afternoon, I believe, that the peace treaty was signed. One thing that surprised me for the three days that I had been in Tokyo Bay before the peace treaty was signed, was the attitude of the Japanese people. They were very friendly, very peaceful, and very nice people.

Q: It's hard to understand, isn't it?

Grant: Yes, especially since they had been defeated. One would think that they would have a grudge against the United States.

Q: And the city at that particular point had been very badly bombed.

Grant: It had been. It had been burned out and also Hiroshima and Nagasaki, which incidentally I flew over about a couple of weeks after the bombing. I had a jeep aboard ship, which I took ashore, and would drive around through the countryside with another officer and just look at the villages and see what the place looked like. The first day we made the trip, there was no sign of

Grant #1 - 54 -

any life in the villages at all. Some of them had been bombed, — the ones which had factories, etc. some of them not, but even the villages that had not been bombed were completely devoid of any life --nothing. The second day we went there and made the same trip through the same villages, a few little children would come out and where they learned the word gum and candy at that time I don't know, but they would come out with their hands out saying, "Gum, candy." Once in awhile we'd see a face of an old man or woman peeking out from behind the house and when they saw that we didn't kill the children, they became a little more friendly. The third time I went there, the older people were out to greet us, and they bowed very ceremoniously, and some who could speak English were very happy that they could speak English and talk to us --very, very friendly.

Q: How do you account for that?

Grant: I guess they're sort of fatalistic people. Maybe it's their religion, I really don't know. They just accept things as they are and try to make the best of them. The emperor had prepared them, I think. I remember I couldn't help thinking that if in San Fransisco we had been attacked and over-run by the Japanese, if any of the Japanese people came in a jeep alone, back up in the hills somewhere, they would have been shot dead. It was a very interesting three weeks. I stayed there for about six months in Tokyo Bay. Of course, after the peace signing ceremonies, or the day before, all sorts of ships came in there --battleships, cruisers, destroyers, aircraft carriers-- but we still had the job of patrolling all around the Japanese islands, the entire coast, all the way up into the Kuriles. We used to go up about a hundred miles in the Kuriles and finally Russia complained. They said they were taking over the Kuriles and we had no business going up there at all. So from then on we got orders to go up only as far north as Hokkaido.

It was quite interesting and I met some very nice Japanese. In fact, I renewed acquaintance with a Japanese boy with whom I had gone to school at Lawrenceville. His father was a Count and he was a member of the Diet and he was rather looked down upon by the rest of the Japanese because he had been all over the world-- he had been international president of the Red Cross at one time-- and he knew perfectly well that Japan had no business making war against the United States because the United States could win the war --not because we had more or braver soldiers, but because we had an economic base which was much better than the Japanese.

One interesting incident occurred with this friend of mine from Japan, with whom I had gone to school -- I'd known him in Lawrenceville, and then he went to Princeton, then over to Oxford and Cambridge and came back and had a job on Wall Street for awhile, and had gotten married in the United States. In fact, his father brought his bride over to Wall Street. One day Chuji Kabayama, my friend, got a call from San Francisco saying in effect, "Son, I brought your bride over and I want you to make arrangements tomorrow for a wedding. I'm flying across." Chuji said, "Papa, who is she?" Papa said, "Well, she's so and so. You remember the family, we've known them for years, and we decided that our families ought to get together so I'm bringing her over and I want you to marry her tomorrow." So Chuji said, "Yes, Papa."

So they got married the next day. I didn't see the bride in this country at all; they soon went back to Japan. When many years later, I visited Japan, I of course, looked him up --this was after the war when I was on the CUMBERLAND SOUND in Tokyo. I didn't look him up right away because I was still, you might say, sort of mad at the Japanese and I wanted to be friends with my friend, so I waited quite a while. Finally I did look him up and he was very happy to see me and invited me down to his place. He had a big place in Oiso, which is just south of Tokyo, and he and his father were there alone for dinner --no wife and children. I knew he had a wife and children but neither his wife nor his children were present. Just the three of us had dinner together. So he invited me back for the next weekend, and the same thing, just the three of us --no wife, no children. The third weekend, just before dinner was announced --they were very western in their customs, we had bourbon, scotch and water, before dinner-- he asked me if I would like to go to the little boy's room. I said I thought it might be a good idea, so he clapped his hands and a screen in the side of the wall opened and a very beautiful Japanese lady was standing there in her long kimono with her hands in her sleeves, and bowed very ceremoniously, and Chuji turned to me and said, by way of introduction, "My wife will now escort you to the toilet." That was the first time I had ever met his wife.

Grant #1 - 57 -

Apparently I behaved myself on the way to the toilet and back, because from then on she always had dinner with us whenever I was there.

Q: After you returned from Japan, you had several duties ashore and in July of '49 went out as commanding officer, naval air station at Agana, Guam, where you were in command of Fleet Air Wing I.

Grant: When the Korean War started in 1950, I was in command of Fleet Air Wing I with headquarters at the naval station at Guam. I had previously been in command of the air station. The Wing was composed of four squadrons --two PBM sea plane squadrons used mainly for patrolling and reconnaissance work, two P2V land plane squadrons used for patrol and reconnaissance work also but in addition were capable of carrying several hundred pounds of bombs over long distances. It was one of the P2V5's that made the world's record long distance flight from Perth on the western coast of Australia to Dayton, Ohio. That's a long distance for one plane to fly.

The mission of Fleet Air Wing I was to patrol the entire western Pacific (this was at the start of the Korean War) on the lookout for any suspicious Communist plane or ship activity. In order to carry out that task most effectively, we had our squadrons widely dispersed. Two were based in Guam, one in the Philippines, and one in Japan. From each of those bases they flew reconnaissance patrols daily, covering most of the strategic areas in the western Pacific Ocean.

On fifteen July, I flew to Okinawa and set up headquarters for the Wing on the Air Force base at Naha. We continued to fly reconnaissance patrols concentrating mainly on the coast of China from near Shanghai on the north to as far as Hong Kong on the south. We paid particular attention to the Formosa Straits and kept the coast from Fuchou south to Swatow, that is the coast just west of Formosa. We kept this area under continuous surveillance twenty-four hours a day. Our principal mission was to be on the lookout for any concentration of ships or aircraft headed from the mainland of China towards Formosa. The government of Formosa was quite worried and feared a Communist invasion any day. The Western Pacific U.S. Naval Command was in Japan and we were to report any suspicious sightings directly to them. The Communists had practically no large naval craft or aircraft but a fleet of five or six hundred large junks could make a rather formidable landing force on the beaches of western Formosa.

In order to establish closer liaison with the Chiang Kai-shek government, I was ordered to Formosa toward the end of July. I severed, temporarily, all connections with Fleet Air Wing I and turned over command to my chief staff officer. I became the senior U.S. naval officer present in Formosa.

Q: Where did you live when you were there?

Grant: I lived in the Princess Hotel. It was on a hill right near where Chiang Kai-shek lived. This was a rather small place. (My wife and I went back there a few years ago by ship. We landed at Kee Lung and took a taxi over and I showed her the Princess Hotel; it had changed quite a bit since I had been there.) I had lived there for about six weeks, I guess. I remember it was only something like twenty-eight dollars a week. Very nice accommodations, the only trouble was there was no hot water in my room. I had to take a cold shower every morning -- a cold bath instead of warm. I finally got used to it but I never got used to liking it.

My principal duties there were to promote friendly relations with the Formosan military and the government in general. I had a few meetings with the generalissimo and they were very interesting. He was very interested in what we were doing to protect Formosa. I remained there about six weeks and was then relived and ordered to return to Okinawa. By that time a sea plane tender was made available to me as my flag ship and I moved my headquarters from the Air Force base at Naha at the southwestern tip of the island to Buckner Bay on the east coast where the ship was anchored.

For the most part the reconnaissance patrols were more or less routine. On occasions however, one of our planes would be followed at a distance by small Communist fighter craft, Chinese Communist fighter craft. In one or two instances, one of our planes would be shot down. Our patrol planes were, of course, no match for a fighter plane. We had orders not to fire unless fired upon. After our first plane had been lost in

Grant # 1 - 60 -

("unless ordered otherwise")

this manner, I gave orders to open fire first whenever an enemy plane was in such a position that it could fire upon one of our planes. We lost only one plane after that. On one or two occasions, sometimes during daylight, sometimes at night, we would spot huge numbers of junks, numbering in the hundreds, setting out from the mainland heading east toward Formosa. We reported them to our destroyers, who were also patrolling the Straits and they would follow them. In each case, however, after the junks would get thirty or forty miles from shore, they would turn around and return. We didn't know whether they were merely on some sort of maneuvers or it was intended as an invasion but they were frightened off by the presence of our aircraft and destroyers.

In March of '51, I was transferred from the command of Fleet Air Wing I and ordered to Moffett Field in command of Fleet Air Detachment. In August of the same year, I was detached from Moffet Field and ordered to the National War College in Washington, D.C. In June of '52, when I graduated, I was ordered to the office of the National Security Affairs in the office of the Secretary of Defense in the Pentagon, where I remained until I retired in 30, June, 1956.

Q: Could you tell me some specific items of interest that occurred during your four years of duty in the office of Secretary of Defense. You were always in foreign affairs, or the Asian Bureau. First, why were you there so long?

Grant # 1 - 61 -

Grant: I was there so long because I knew I was going to retire, or at least I thought I was going to retire, in '56 and I didn't want to leave there in three years and have just one tour of duty somewhere else, unless it was sea duty. I was offered a job somewhere as a naval instructor in some college in the Middle West but I turned that down. So I stayed on until I retired. While in the Department of Defense I traveled around a little bit. I went to Europe and Turkey and a few places where they had international meetings but nothing especially interesting.

Q: How did you know you were going to retire at the end of four years?

Grant: Because I had been passed over in '54, which means that in two years I would retire. I didn't want to go anywhere else. We owned a home in Arlington, Virginia. I thought I might as well stay there until it was all over with, and then I knew perfectly well I was going back to California because there's no place like Ca-ifornia.

Q: Do you feel you should have been selected for admiral?

Grant: Oh no. I was too easy going. I didn't bawl people out enough. I'm sort of exaggerating, of course, but I was too easy going.

Q: What people can you identify as having the most influence in your life in the Navy?

Grant: That's hard to say. There were so many very nice, very wonderful senior officers whom I ran into and tried to be like, and others the opposite, whom I decided I certainly wasn't going to be like. I really don't have any special hero who stands out.

Q: Do you feel your years in the Navy were successful ones?

Grant: Oh yes. I really wouldn't have changed a thing. When I graduated from Lawrenceville, or before, my father wanted me to go to Princeton and study economics; he wanted me to be a banker and come in with him. When this chance came to go to Annapolis, I had always liked the sea and I'd always liked sailing and boating, I decided I couldn't pass that up. I think it was sort of a disappointment to my father that I did.

INDEX

to Interview with

JAMES ETHERIDGE GRANT
Rear Admiral, U. S. Navy (Ret.)

Alice Springs, 31.

Australians - attitude towards Americans, 42-43

Balikpapan, 9-10

Buton, 20; attitude of population, 21-22

Carnarvon, 40

Chicago - CA, 37

Childs - seaplane tender, 13, 39

Cumberland Sound - seaplane tender, 48; commissioning, 49; patrols off Kwajalein, 50; off Ulithi, 51

Darwin, 13, 18, 23, 40, includes account of only air raid during WW II; U. S. Consul turns over command in face of air raid, 29-30

Exmouth Gulf, 39-40, 46

Fleet Air Wing I, mission at outset of Korean War, 57-58

Formosa (Taiwan), 58; reconnaissance patrols, 59

Fremantle, 33, 39, 42

Grant, RADM Etheridge: counter-spy duty, 43ff; as pearl fisherman, 46-47; duties before and after surrender in Tokyo Bay, 51-52; meeting with Admiral Nimitz, 52; observations on Japanese people after surrender, 53-57

Guam - Grant in command there of Fleet Air Wing I, 57

Jacksonville, 48

Kendari Bay, 16, 20

Makassar, 11

Missouri, BB, 52-53

Moffett Field, 60

Moorer, Admiral Thomas, 21, 40ff; includes incident where his plane shot down, 41-42

National War College, 60

Natives - attitude, N.E.I., 14, in Celebes; native communications, 14, 46

Perth, 32

Philippines, attack on, 3-9; outbreak of World War II

William B. Preston - seaplane tender, 2, 6, 12, 17, 31, 32, 33; repairs in Fremantle, 34; repairs in Sydney, 35-36; replacements, 39; his planes patrol, 40

Saratoga, CV, 2

Soerabaja, 12

Swan, seaplane tender, 10

Sydney: attack on Sydney Harbor by Japanese midget SS's, 36, 37

Tarakan, 10-11

Ulithi, 38, kamikazi attack

Zamboanga, 9-10, 33

www.ingramcontent.com/pod-product-compliance
Lightning Source LLC
Chambersburg PA
CBHW080610170426
43209CB00007B/1386